YOU BETTER WATCH OUT
THE WISDOM OF SANTA

THE ENTHUSIAST

The Enthusiast publishes books and paper goods. Subjects include, vintage how-to, retro-cooking and home economics, holidays and celebrations, games and puzzles, graphic design, classic children's literature, illustrated literature and poetry, humour.

What's Your Passion?

 Enthusiast.cc

 TheEnthusiast@Enthusiast.cc

Copyright, 2015, by
The Enthusiast
All rights reserved - no part of this book may be reproduced in any form without permission in writing from the publisher.

ISBN / EAN
1595838635 / 978-1595838636

There are amongst us certain persons who do not believe in the existence of Santa Claus. Apparently there is not enough evidence for them. Or they have not seen Santa with their own eyes. In some cases, discovering their parents acting on Santa's behalf, they began to doubt. For those of us who do believe in Santa this is a lamentable state of affairs, we want everyone to share in the joy that Santa brings the world each and every Christmas. Thus we have attempted in this book to prove the reason and existence of Santa Claus using his own words and those of his close friends and confidantes. If we convert but one Grinch to belief in Santa it will have been worth it. To quote Bart Simpson, "Hey, since when is Christmas just about presents? Aren't we forgetting the true meaning of this day... the birth of Santa? "

- The Enthusiast

In all this world there is nothing so beautiful as a happy child.

Life and Adventures of Santa Claus
by L. Frank Baum

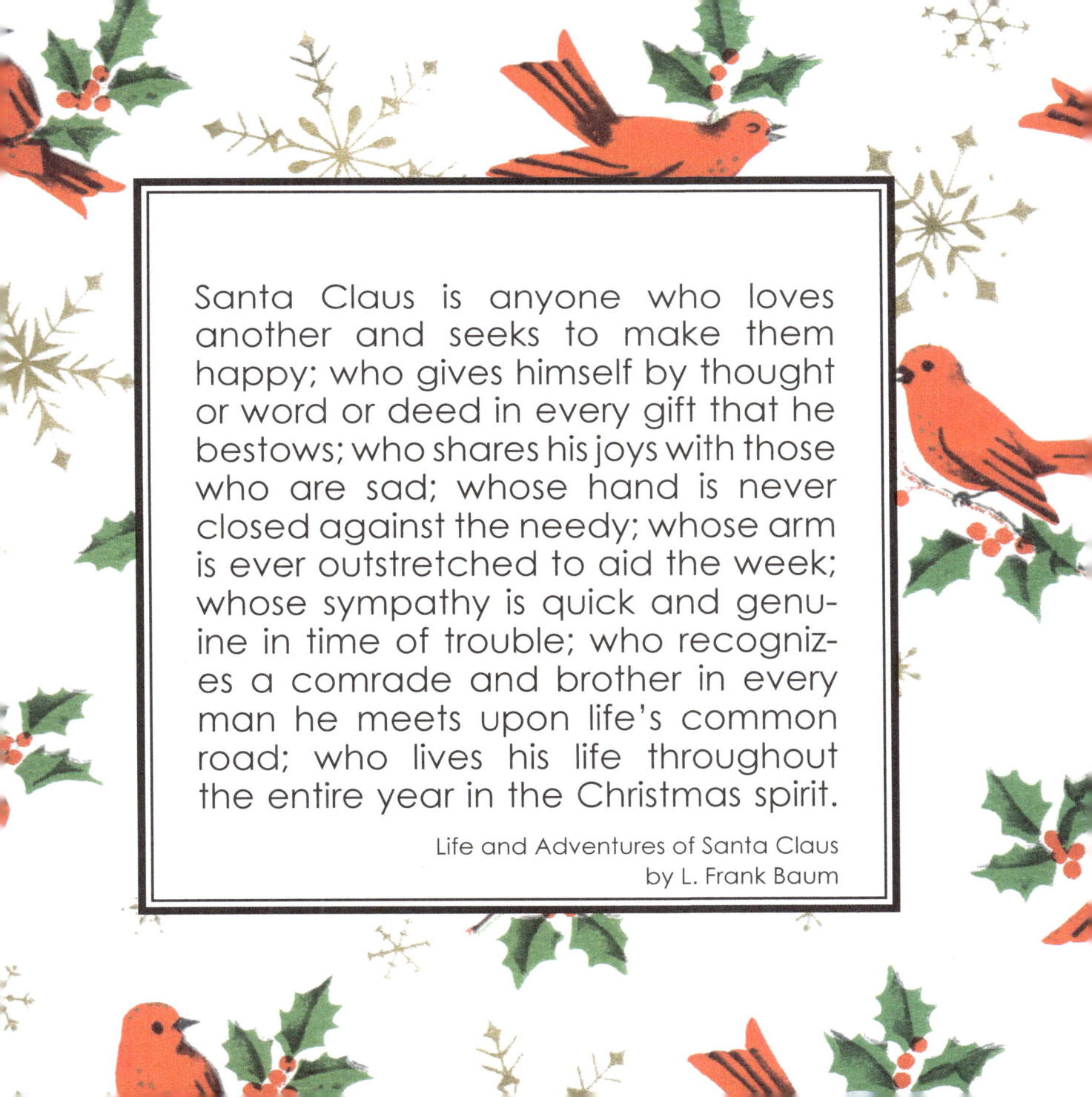

Santa Claus is anyone who loves another and seeks to make them happy; who gives himself by thought or word or deed in every gift that he bestows; who shares his joys with those who are sad; whose hand is never closed against the needy; whose arm is ever outstretched to aid the week; whose sympathy is quick and genuine in time of trouble; who recognizes a comrade and brother in every man he meets upon life's common road; who lives his life throughout the entire year in the Christmas spirit.

Life and Adventures of Santa Claus
by L. Frank Baum

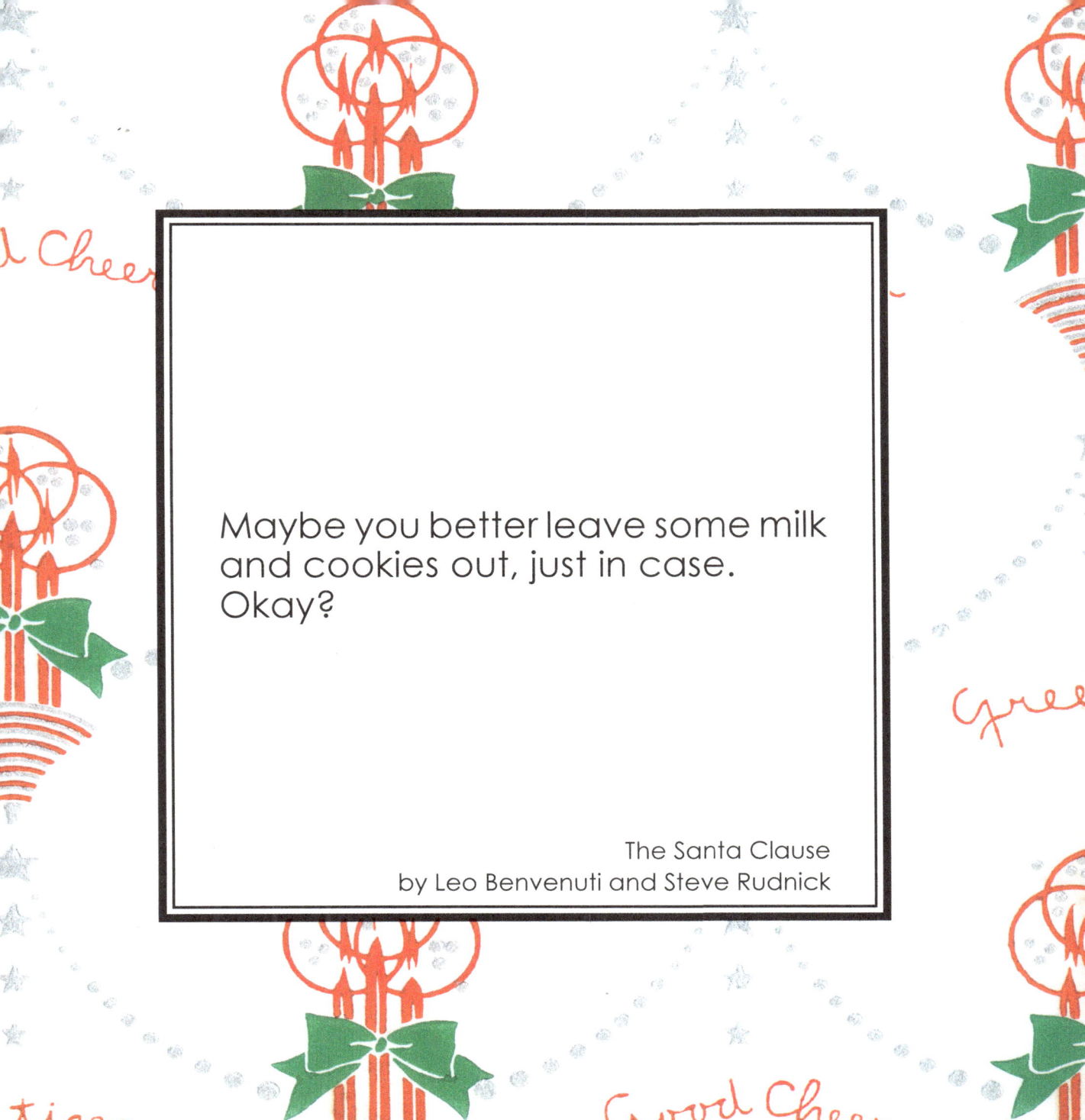

Maybe you better leave some milk and cookies out, just in case. Okay?

The Santa Clause
by Leo Benvenuti and Steve Rudnick

I'm not just a whimsical figure who wears a charming suit and affects a jolly demeanor. You know, I'm a symbol. I'm a symbol of the human ability to be able to suppress the selfish and hateful tendencies that rule the major part of our lives. If you can't believe, if you can't accept anything on faith, then you're doomed for a life dominated by doubt.

Miracle on 34th Street
by George Seaton and Valentine Davies

Oh, Christmas isn't just a day, it's a frame of mind... and that's what's been changing. That's why I'm glad I'm here, maybe I can do something about it.

Miracle on 34th Street
by George Seaton and Valentine Davies

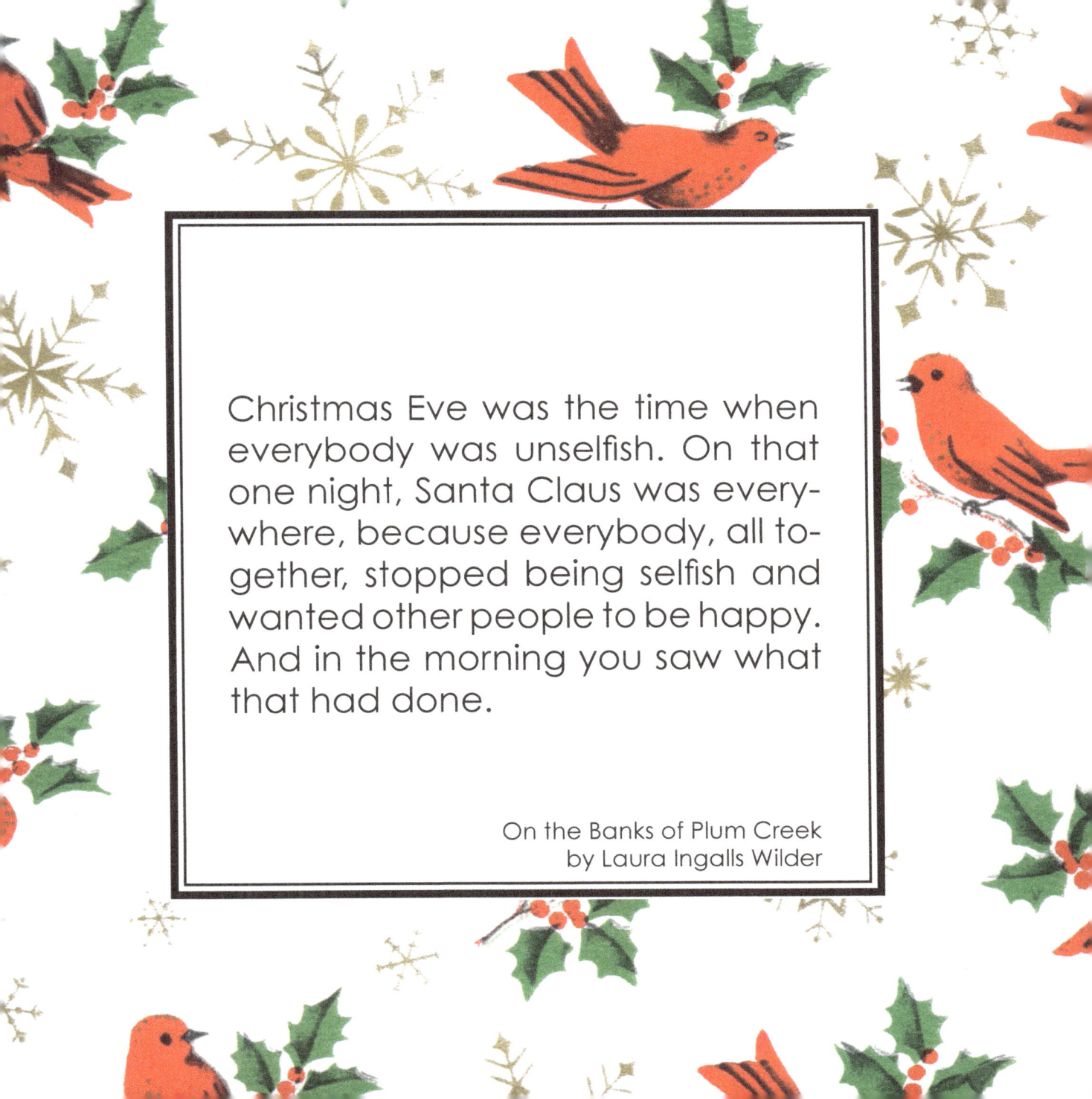

Christmas Eve was the time when everybody was unselfish. On that one night, Santa Claus was everywhere, because everybody, all together, stopped being selfish and wanted other people to be happy. And in the morning you saw what that had done.

On the Banks of Plum Creek
by Laura Ingalls Wilder

Just because every child can't get his wish that doesn't mean there isn't a Santa Claus.

Miracle on 34th Street
by George Seaton and Valentine Davies

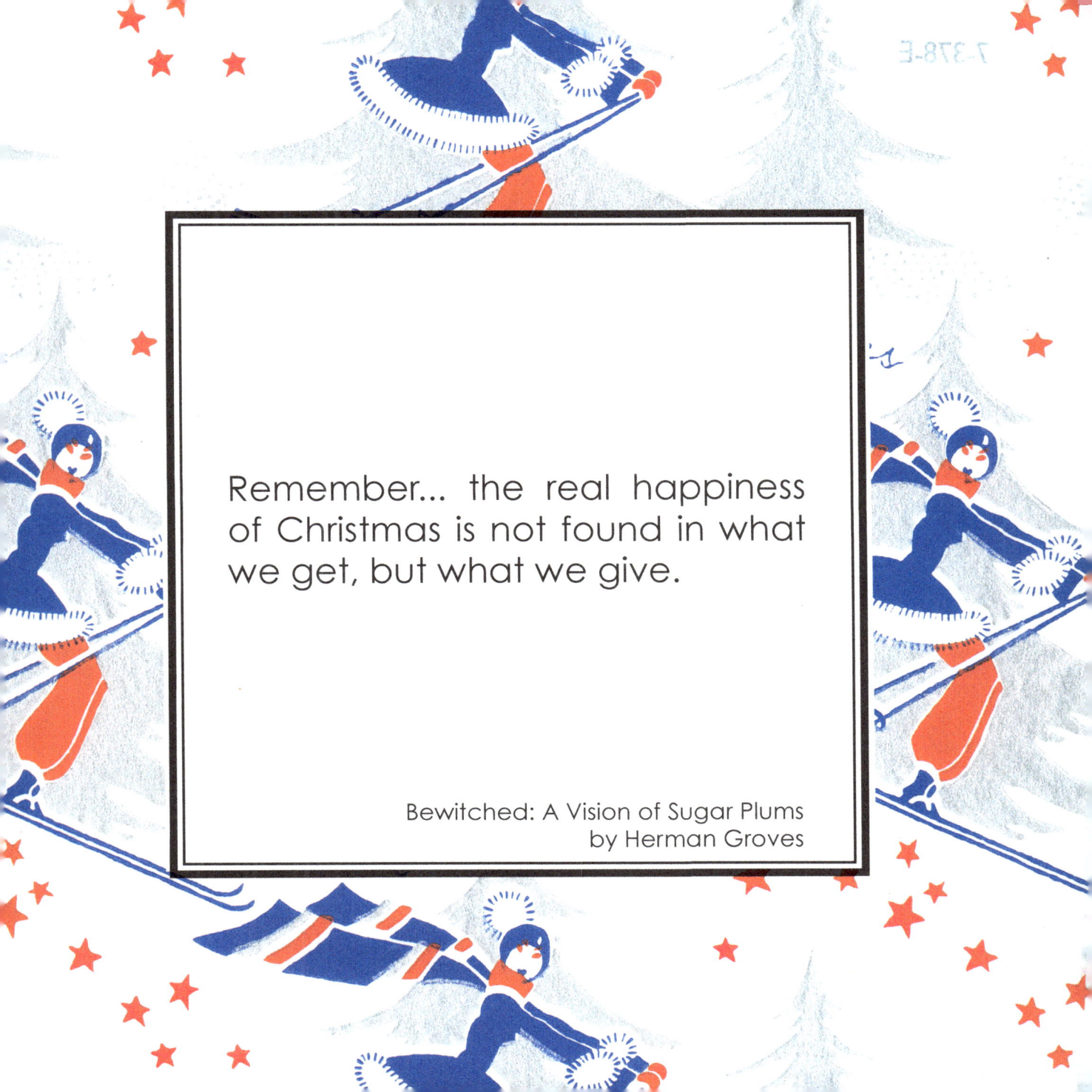

Remember... the real happiness of Christmas is not found in what we get, but what we give.

Bewitched: A Vision of Sugar Plums
by Herman Groves

He sees you when you're sleeping...

...He knows when you're awake

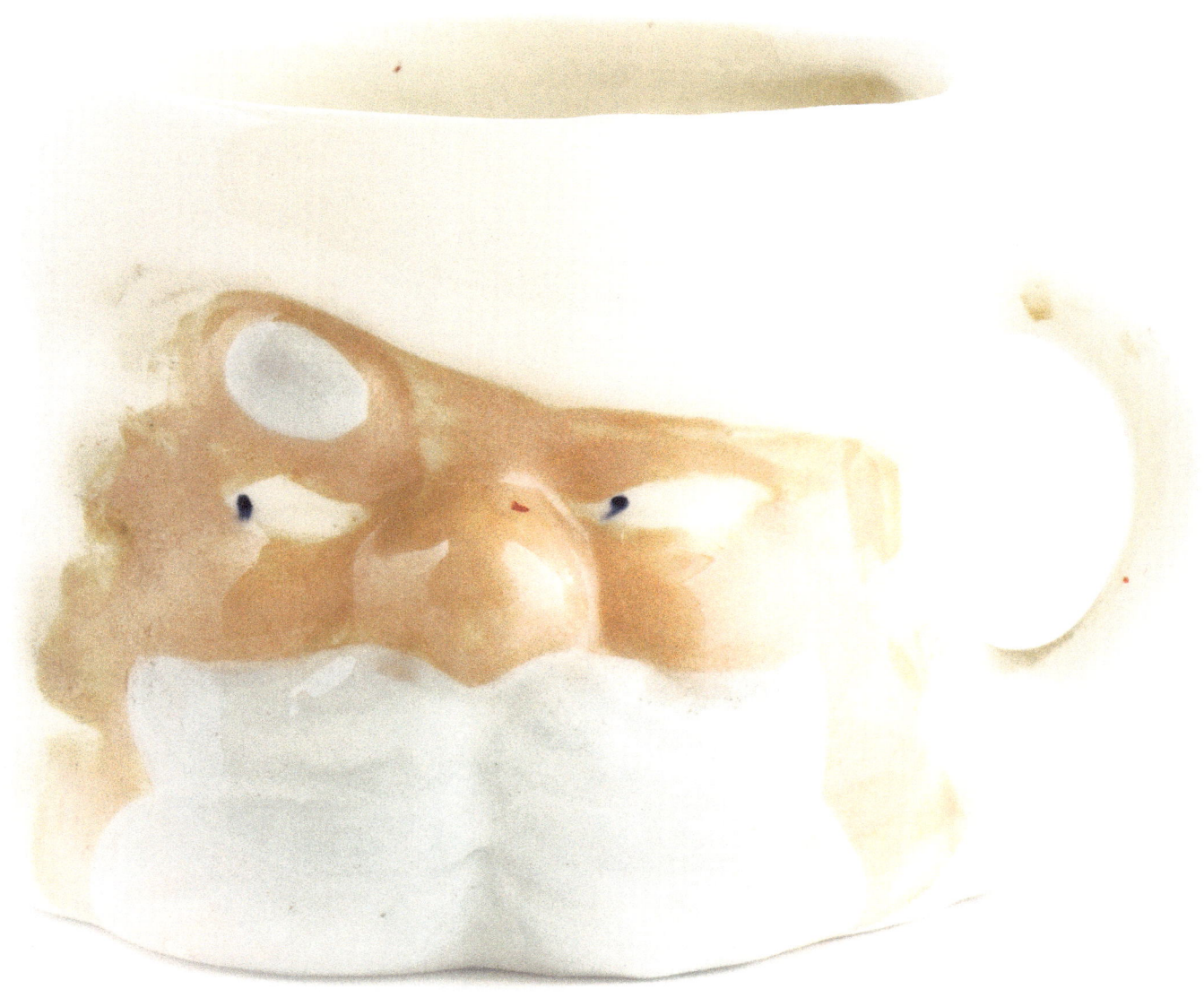

I don't know who started the idea of "naughty or nice", but is wasn't me. Every child gets a gift.

Interviews with Santa Claus
by Welleran Poltarnees

Seeing isn't believing.
Believing is seeing.

The Santa Clause
by Leo Benvenuti and Steve Rudnick

The most real things in the world are those that neither children nor men can see.

Yes, Virginia, there is a Santa Claus
by Francis P. Church

Jingle, jingle, jingle,
You will hear my sleigh bells ring
I am old Kris Kringle
I'm the king of jing-a-ling.

Rudolph, the Red-Nosed Reindeer
by Romeo Muller and Robert May

We love the biting cold, the shining stars and the peace of the world asleep.

Interviews with Santa Claus
by Welleran Poltarnees

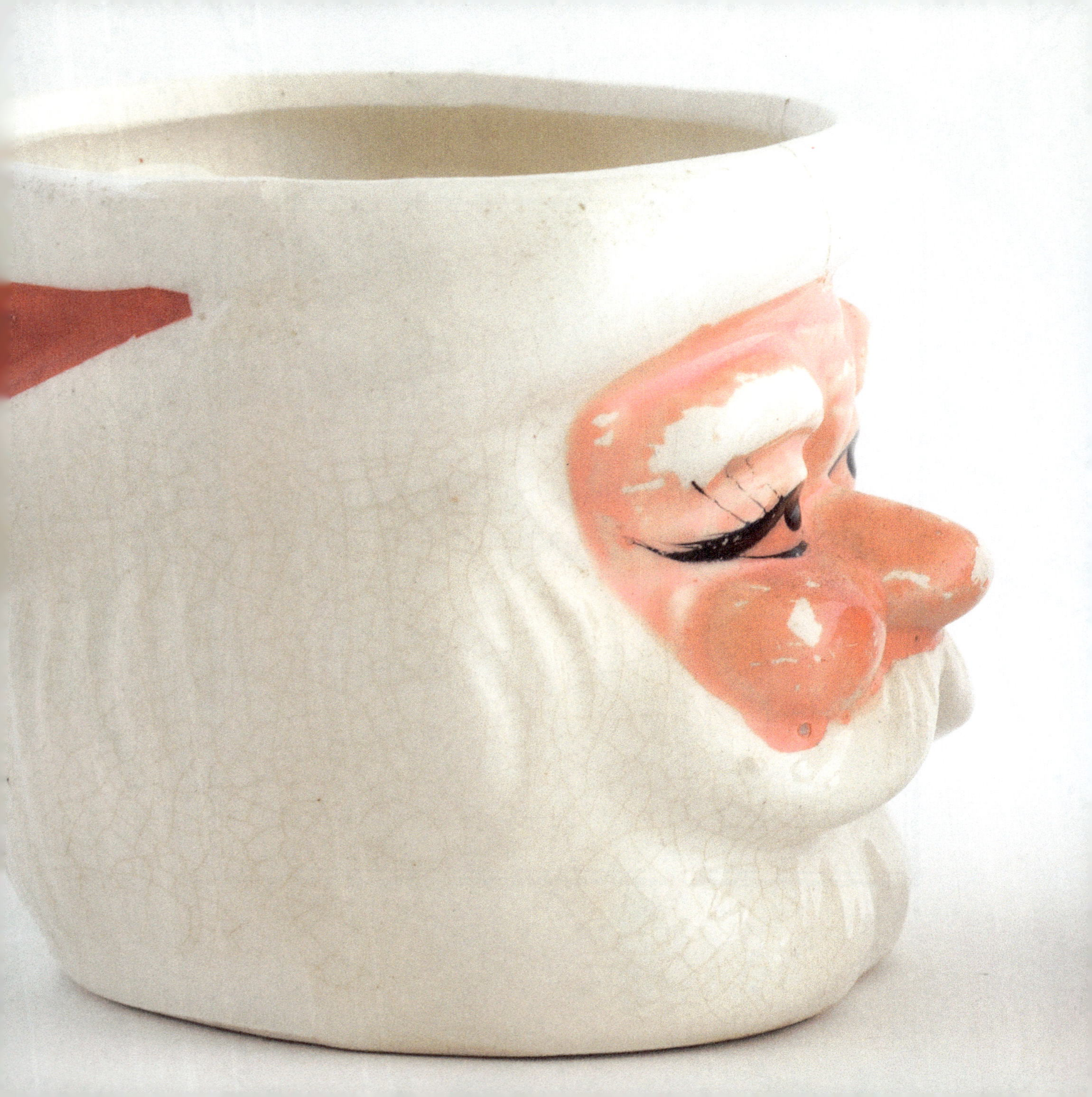

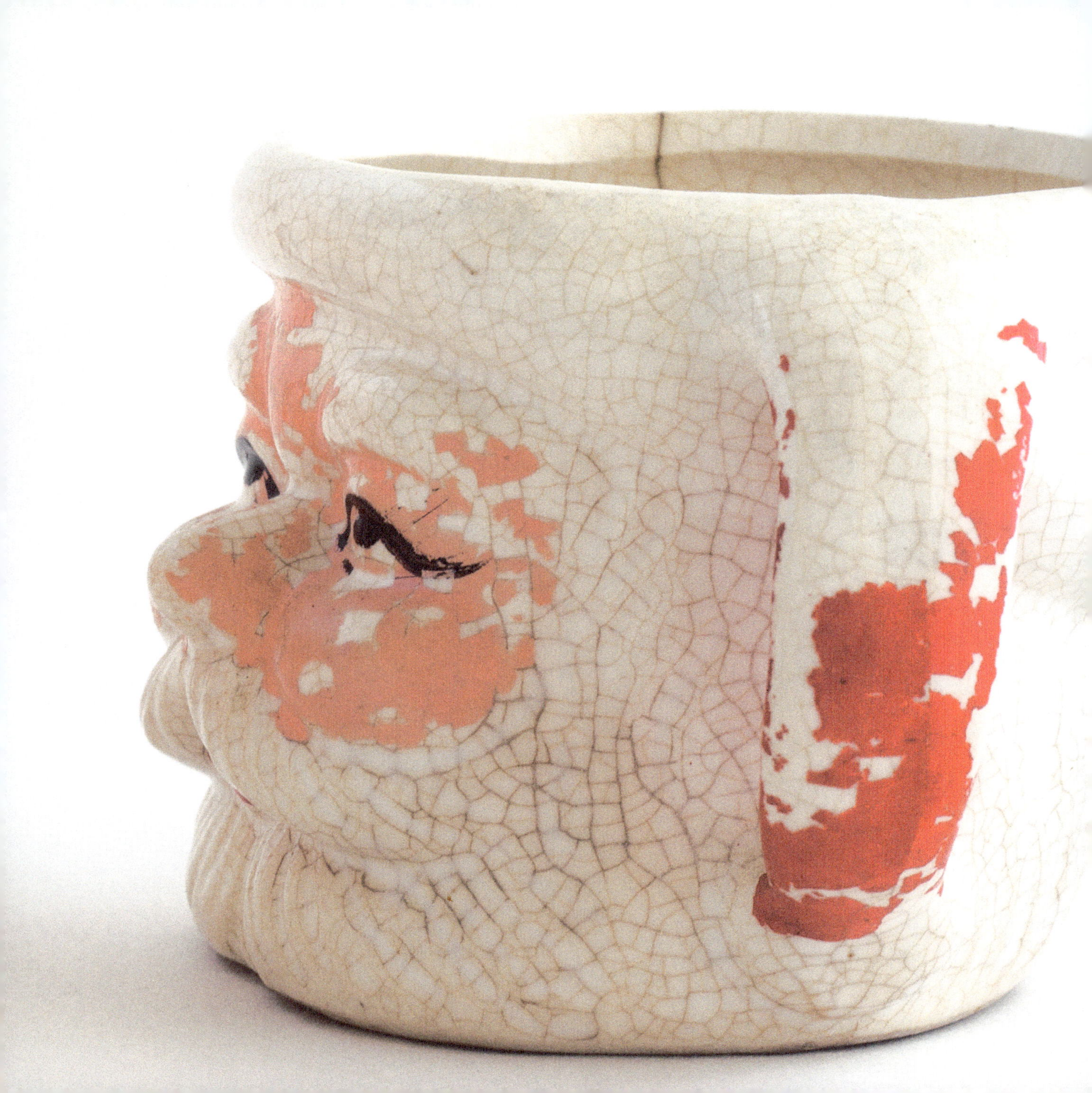

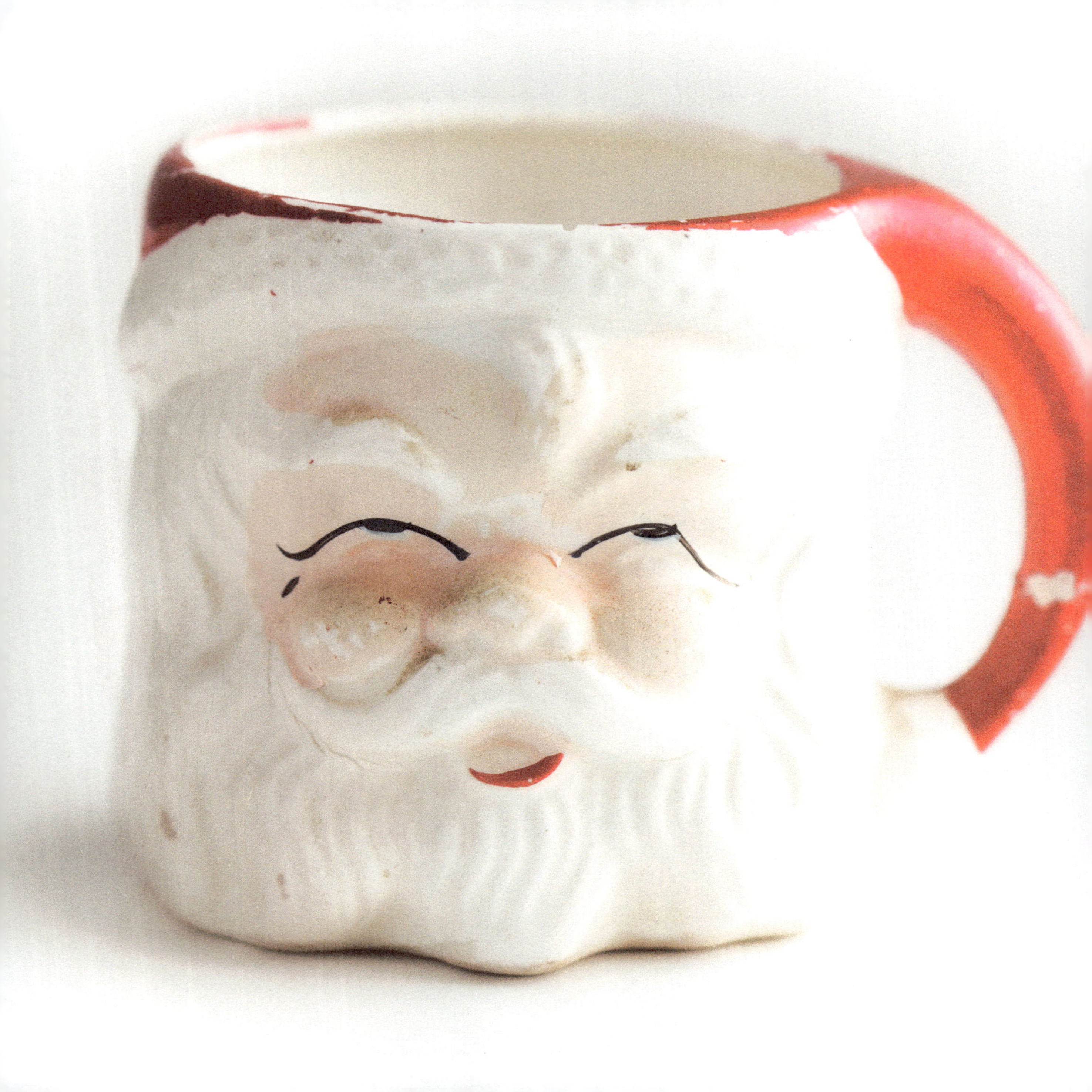

Not believe in Santa Claus! You might as well not believe in fairies! You might get your papa to hire men to watch in all the chimneys on Christmas Eve to catch Santa Claus, but even if they did not see Santa Claus coming down, what would that prove? Nobody sees Santa Claus, but that is no sign that there is no Santa Claus.

Yes, Virginia, there is a Santa Claus
by Francis P. Church

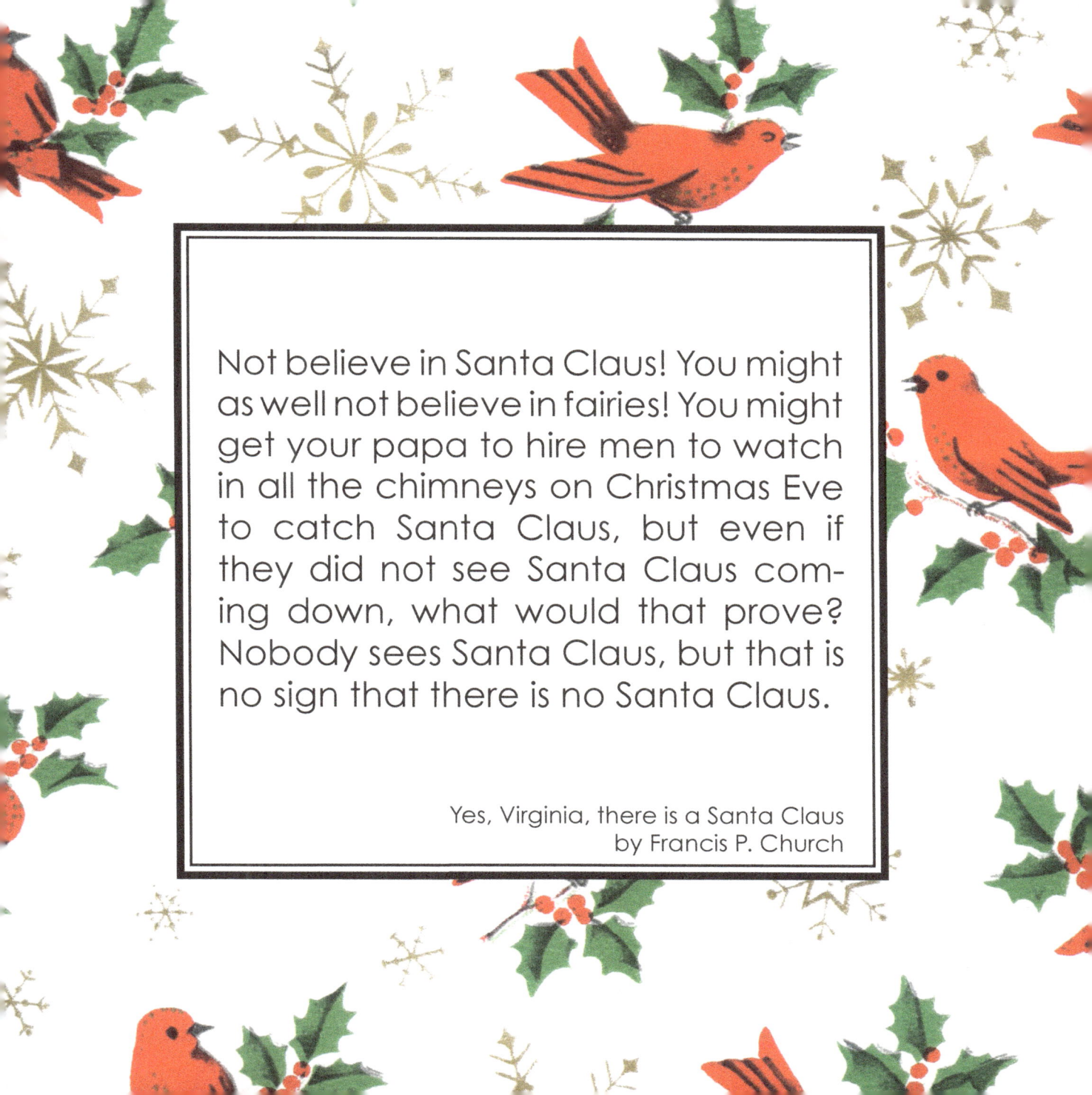

I see all of you!

Interviews with Santa Claus
by Welleran Poltarnees

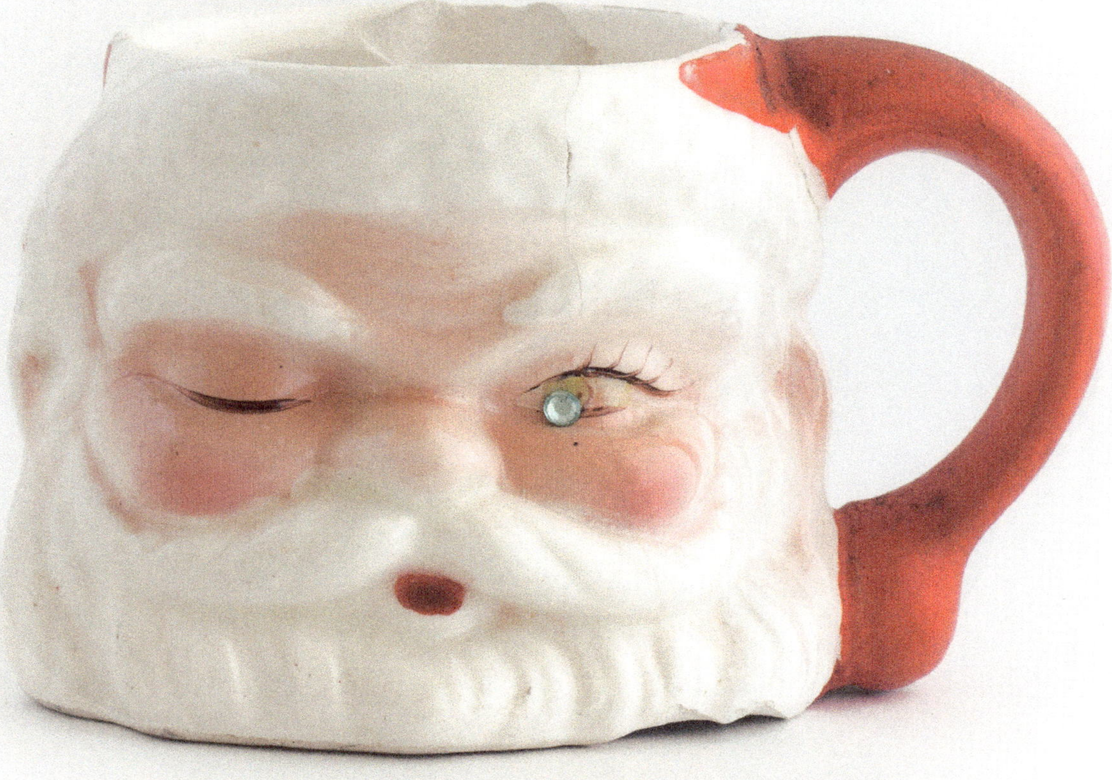

There is a Santa Claus. He exists as certainly as love and generosity and devotion exist...

...and you know that they abound and give to your life its highest beauty and joy.

Yes, Virginia, there is a Santa Claus
by Francis P. Church

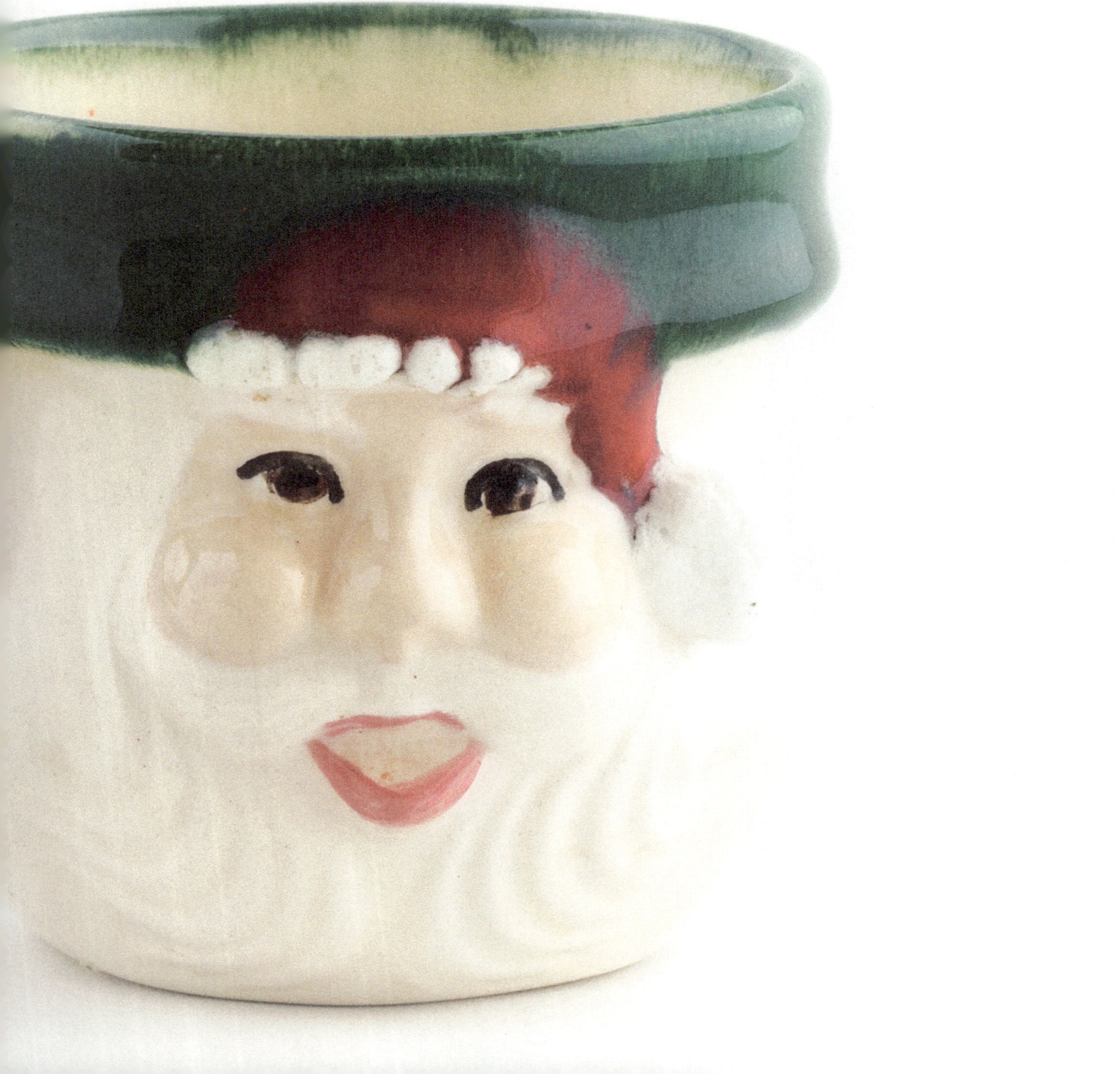

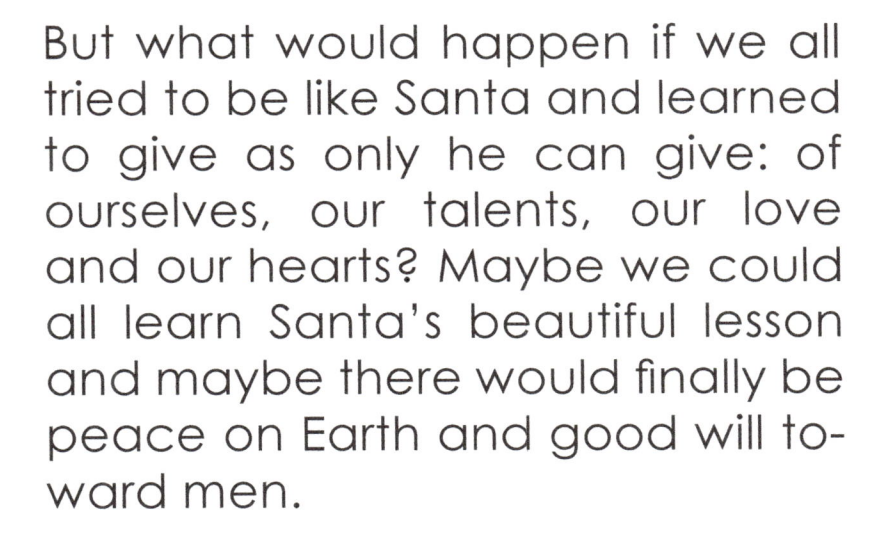

But what would happen if we all tried to be like Santa and learned to give as only he can give: of ourselves, our talents, our love and our hearts? Maybe we could all learn Santa's beautiful lesson and maybe there would finally be peace on Earth and good will toward men.

Santa Claus Is Comin' to Town
by Romeo Muller

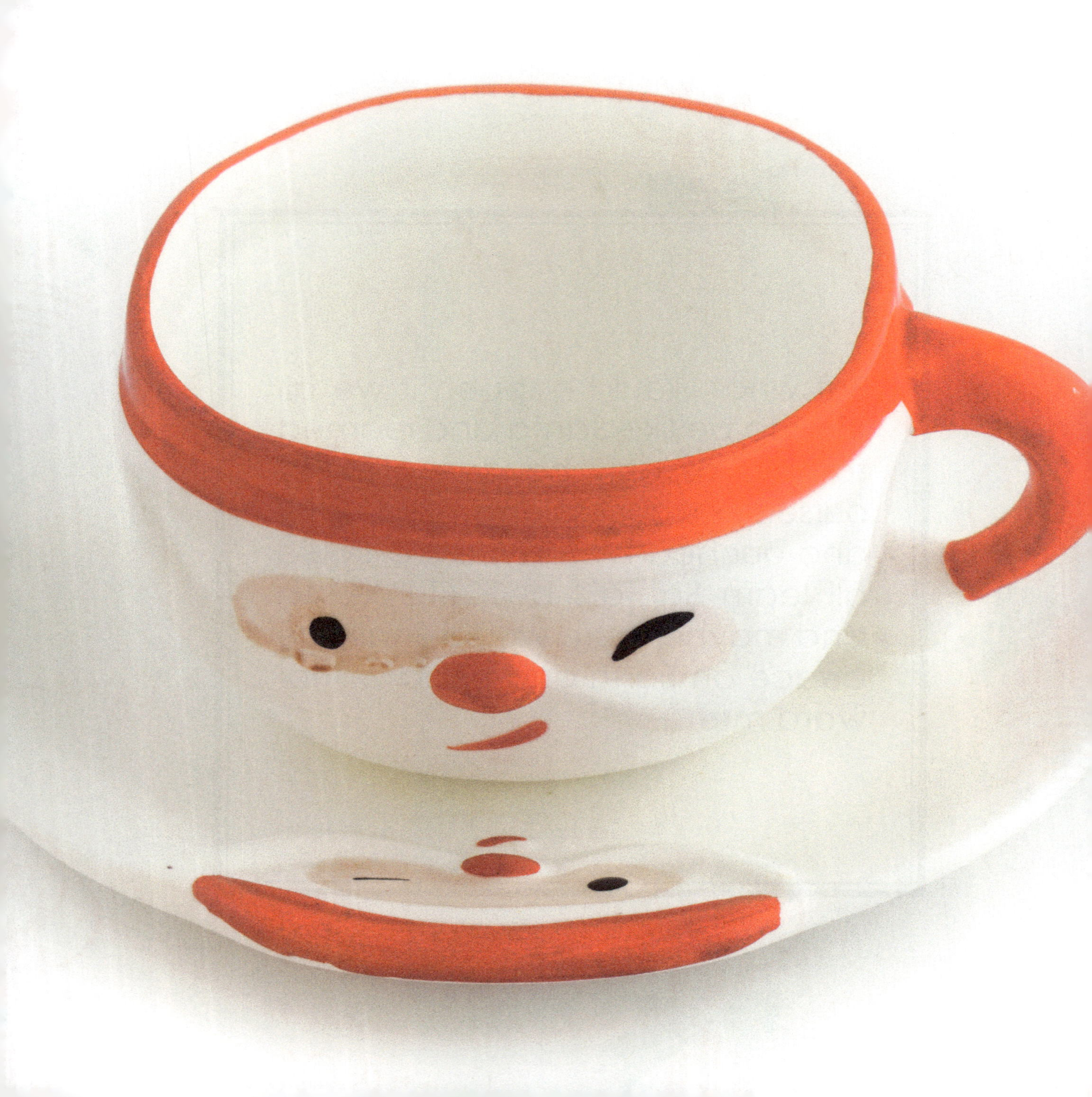

It's hard to explain, but...
giving makes a person feel very, very good.

The Great Santa Claus Switch
by Jerry Juhl

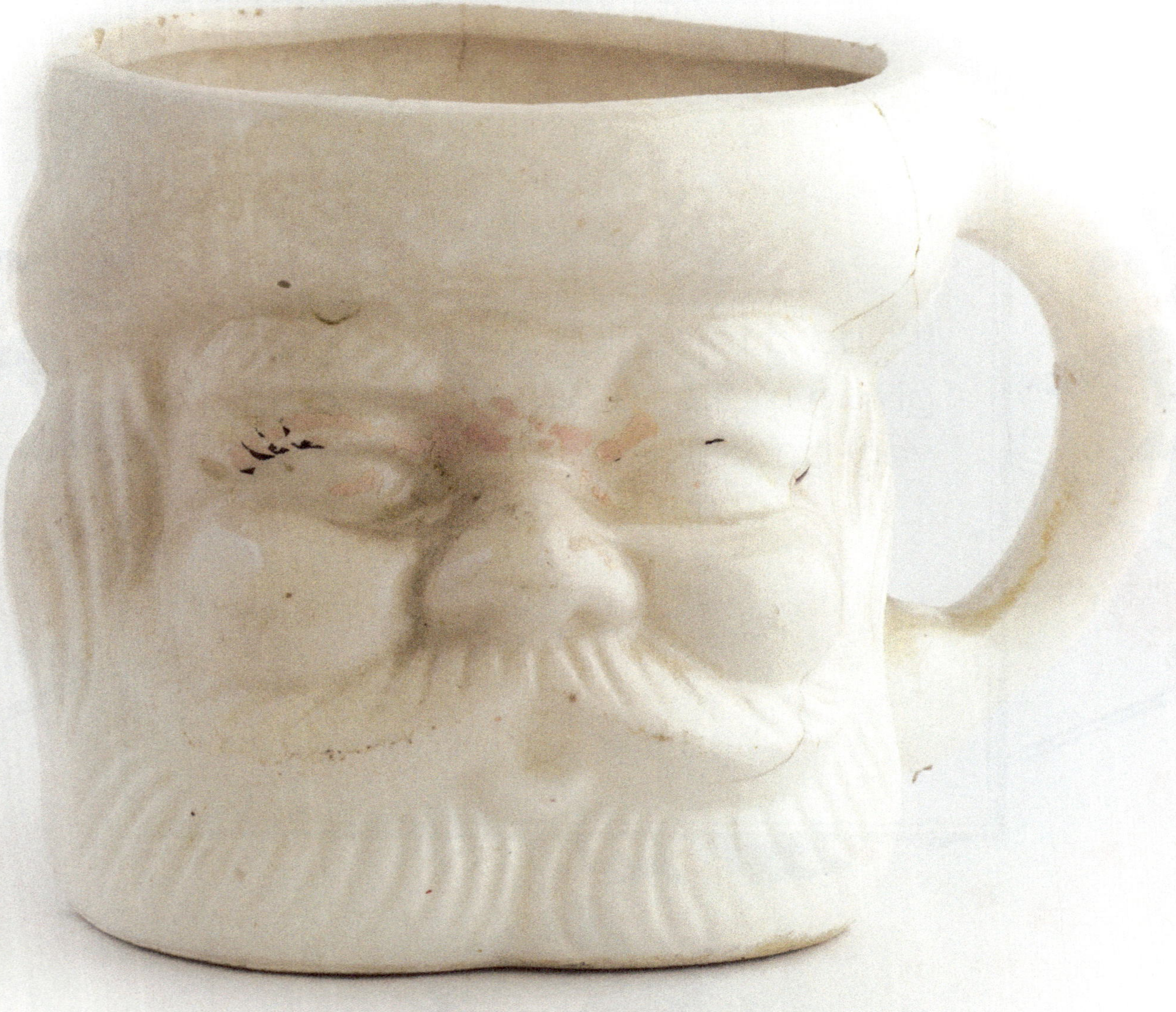

Seeing is believing, but sometimes the most real things in the world are the things we can't see.

Polar Express
by Chris Van Allsburg and Robert Zemeckis

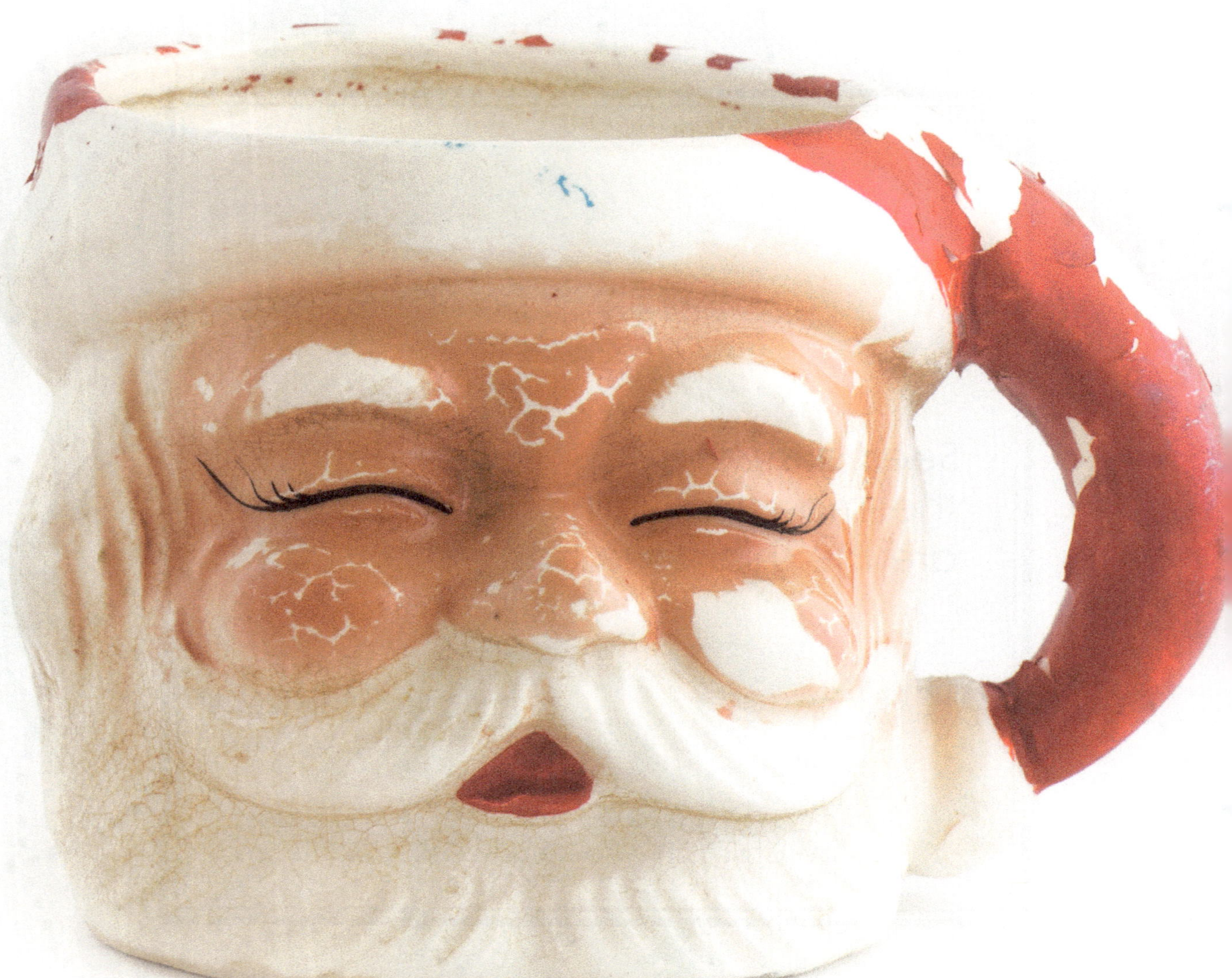

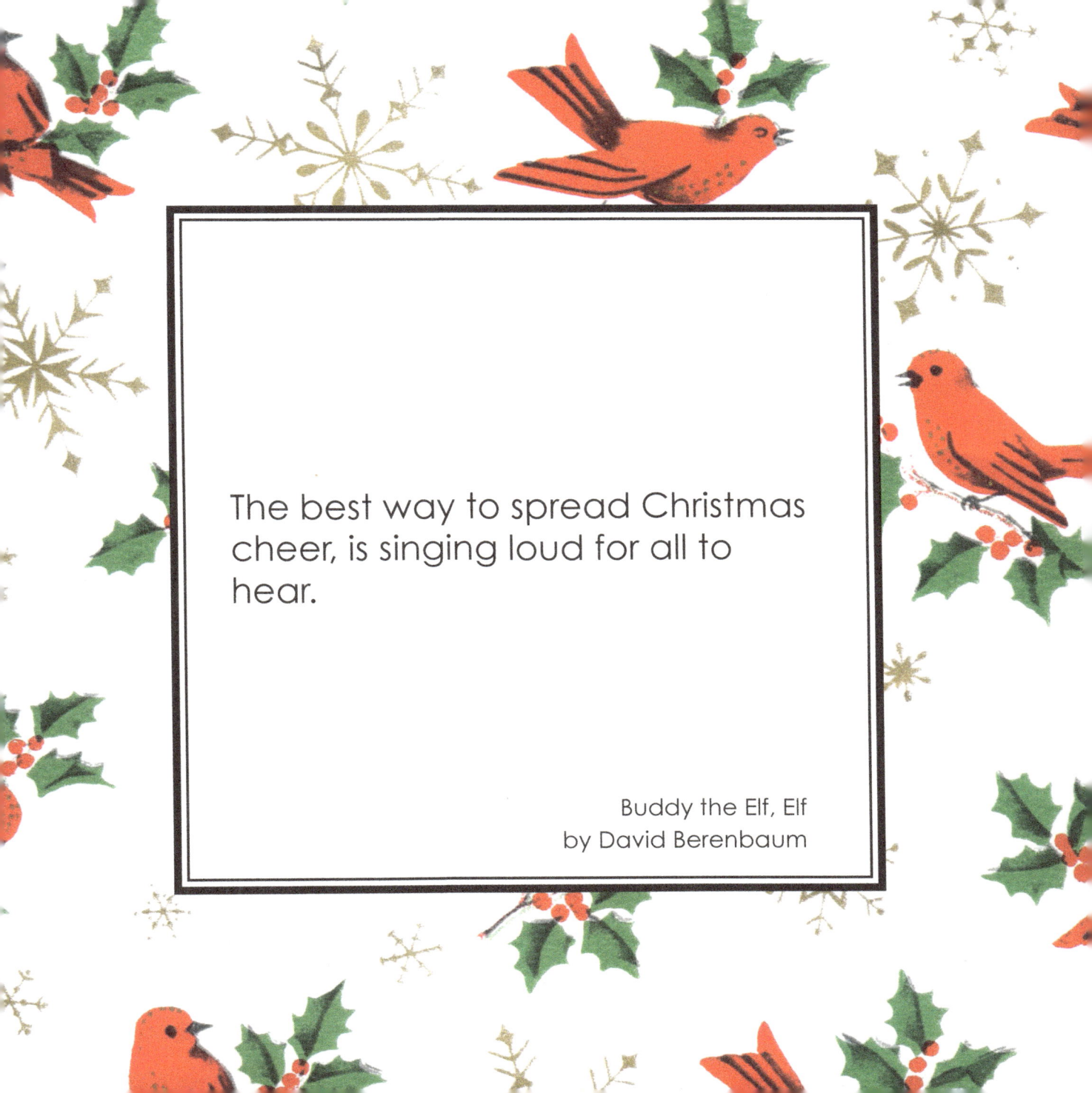

The best way to spread Christmas cheer, is singing loud for all to hear.

Buddy the Elf, Elf
by David Berenbaum

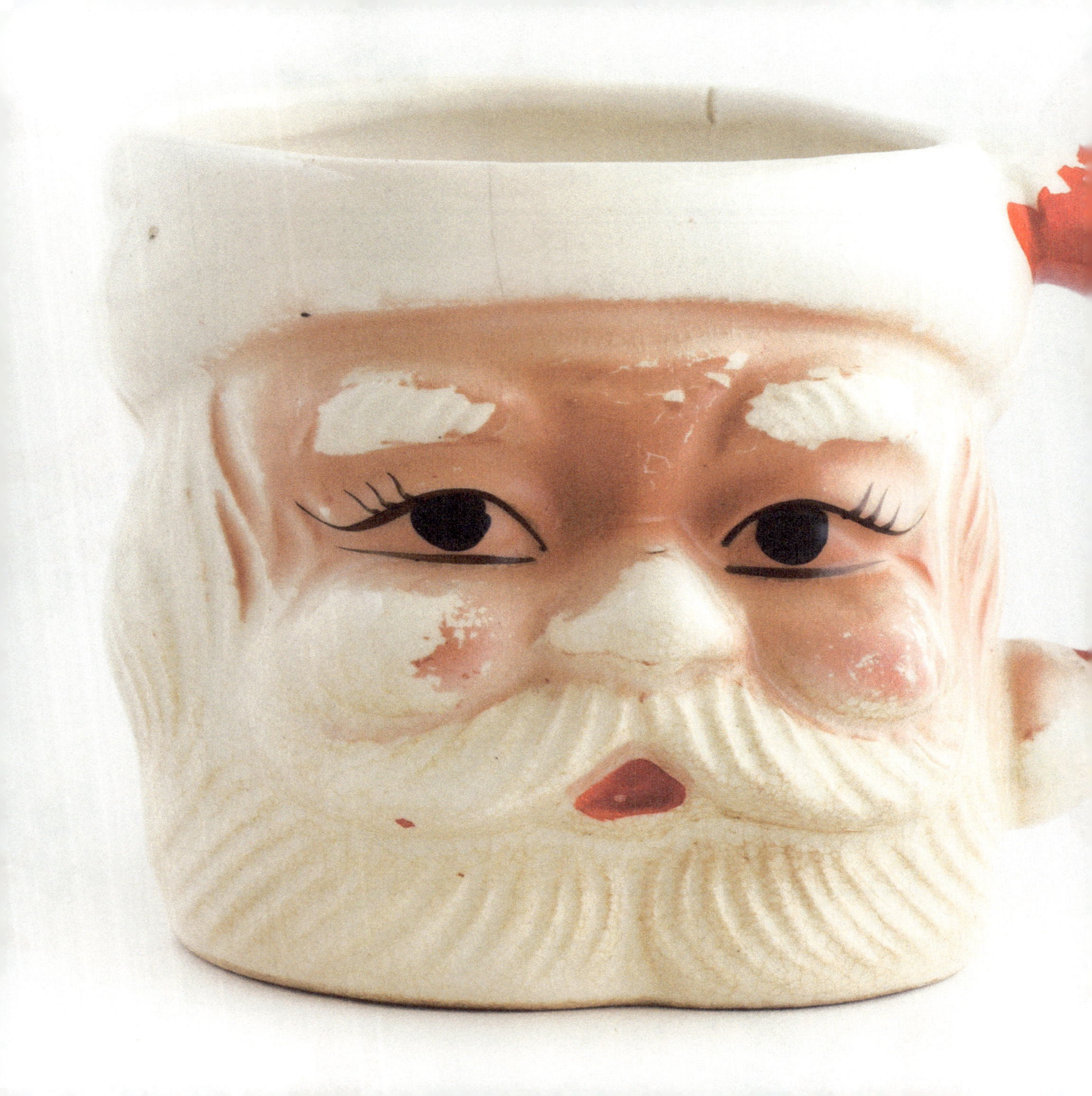

HAPPY CHRISTMAS to ALL and to ALL A GOOD NIGHT!

A Visit from St. Nicholas
by Clement C. Moore

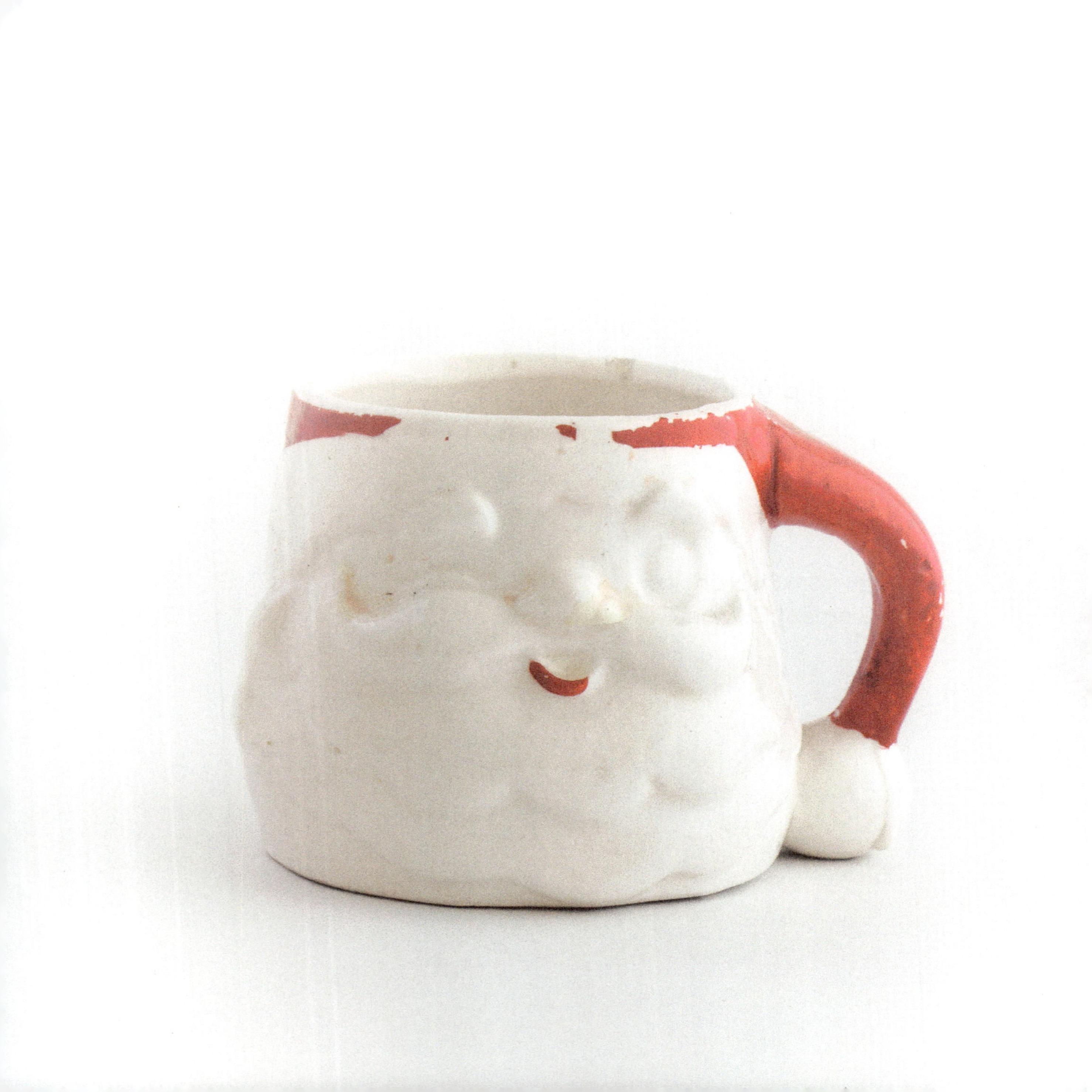

254

Miracle on 34th Street by George Seaton and Valentine Davies, 1947

Santa Claus is Coming to Town by John Frederick Coots and Haven Gillespie, 1934

Bewitched: A Vision of Sugar Plums by Herman Groves, 1964

The Story of Santa Claus by Rachel Koretsky and Steven Whitestone, 1996

The Autobiography of Santa Claus by Jeff Guinn, 2006

Life and Adventures of Santa Claus by L Frank Baum, 1902

My Christmas Gift: A Little Book of Christmas Thoughts by Edwin Osgood Grover, 1912

Santa Claus Is Comin' to Town by Romeo Muller, 1970

The Santa Clause by Leo Benvenuti and Steve Rudnick, 1994

The Simpsons: Miracle on Evergreen Terrace by Ron Hauge, 1997

Elf by David Berenbaum, 2003

Rudolph, the Red-Nosed Reindeer by Romeo Muller, Robert May, 1964

A visit from St. Nicholas by Clement C. Moore, 1823

The Great Santa Claus Switch by Jerry Juhl, 1970

On the Banks of Plum Creek by Laura Ingalls Wilder, 1937

Interviews with Santa Claus by Welleran Poltarnees, unpublished

design Danielle Marshall
photography Sarah Kistner

CPSIA information can be obtained at www.ICGtesting.com
Printed in the USA
LVOW02s1618200415

435344LV00011B/24/P

9 781595 838636